Mothers

Mothers

COURAGE
BOOKS

AN IMPRINT OF RUNNING PRESS
PHILADELPHIA • LONDON

9   8   7   6   5   4   3   2   1
Digit on the right indicates the number of this printing

Library of Congress Cataloging-in-Publication Number 2004107411

ISBN 0-7624-2328-5

Cover and interior design by Corinda Cook
Art researched by Susan Oyama
Introduction by Janet Hendrickson

This book may be ordered by mail from the publisher.
But try your bookstore first!

Published by Courage Books, an imprint of
Running Press Book Publishers
125 South Twenty-second Street
Philadelphia, Pennsylvania 19103-4399

Visit us on the web!
www.runningpress.com

Contents

Introduction

Aeschylus had one. Oedipus had one. Hamlet had one, and so did Napoleon.

And so do you.

What is it?

No surprise—it's a mother. Given the title of this book, even a riddle as hazy as that one isn't hard to answer. It's the kind that only a mother would pretend to guess and laugh at, just like she laughed the first fifteen times her children told a knock-knock joke. Fortunately, we'll try to tell this one only once.

It's hard to write about mothers since so much has already been said. One cliché among the many is that motherhood is the world's oldest profession. Both men and women loved their mothers for ages before Freud picked up on the fact, and probably in ways a little deeper than Freud expected. Mothers held political clout long before a politician lumped a few together and branded them all soccer moms. Mothers inspired many of the proverbs they still pass on. Mothers were muses for many a poem—some of them even good—before Mother's Day greeting cards smothered our affections in a blanket of sentimentality.

Though most of us have known and loved a mother longer than any other person in the world, telling a mother how much we love her can be as daunting as expressing love to anyone else. Fortunately, over the centuries, more than a few people have emerged as articulate while the rest of us feel like we're gurgling the baby talk that only a mother can interpret. Luminaries of all sorts have uttered words of wit and wonder for their mothers that someone, fortunately, thought to write down. Artists, meanwhile, have painted portraits for centuries of the figure of the mother that are far more discernable than our scribbled first-grade efforts mom hung on the fridge.

So, fortunately, when a simple "I love you" doesn't seem like enough, we still don't have to say anything. This book brings together tributes from playwrights and preachers, actresses and feminists, characters famous and fictional. Not all of the sentiment is as sticky as the countertop mom never got us to clean up. For let's be honest, mothers and children do laugh at each other all the time. The images and reflections in this collection capture every range of emotion; from the months the mother waits for the child to be born to the bittersweet arrival of adulthood, where each can exchange words as equals and friends. This volume totals to be a treasury everyone can genuinely appreciate.

Anticipation

When God thought of mother,
He must have laughed with satisfaction,
and framed it quickly—so rich,
so deep, so divine, so full of soul, power,
and beauty, was the conception.

—Henry Ward Beecher

(1813–1887)

American cleric

I begin to love this little creature and to anticipate his birth as a fresh twist to a knot which I do not wish to untie.

—Mary Wollstonecraft

(1759–1797)

British writer

"You are the caretaker of the generations,
you are the birth giver," the sun told the woman.
"You will be the carrier of the universe."

—Brule Sioux,

Sun Creation Myth

This was an initiation,

through which I experienced a profound kinship with all women throughout history who had ever gone through this ordeal and transformation. There was nothing that distinguished me from any woman who had ever given birth to a baby.

—Jean Shinoda Bolen

(b. 1936)

American writer and psychiatrist

. . . It is still the biggest gamble in the world.
It is the glorious life force.
It's huge and scary—it's an act of infinite optimism.

—Gilda Radner

(1946–1989)

American comedian

Newborns

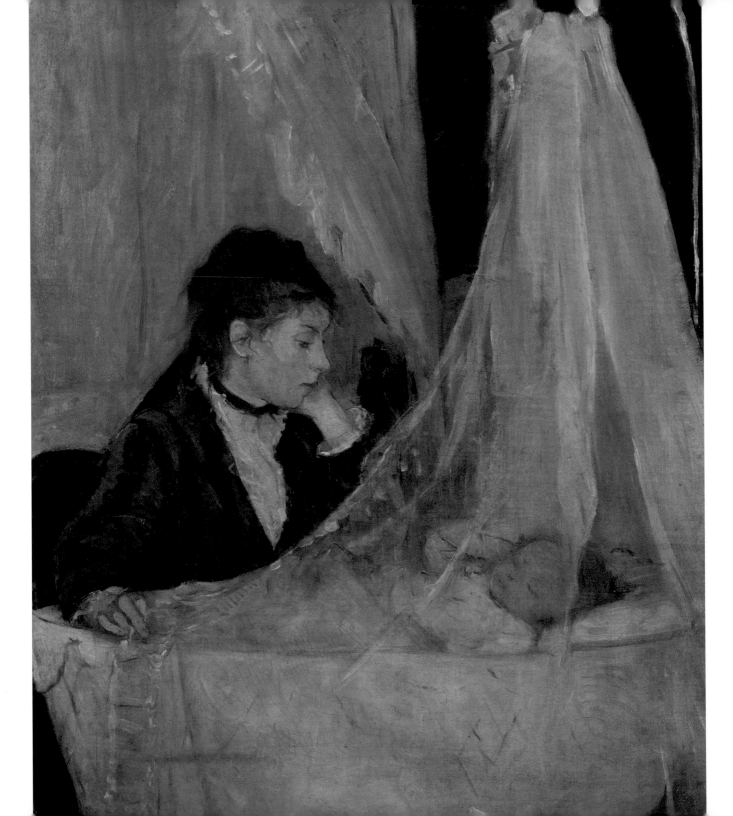

There is an

amazed curiosity

in every

young mother.

It is strangely

miraculous to see

and to hold a

living being formed

within oneself

and issued forth

from oneself.

—Simone de Beauvoir

(1908–1986)

French writer

It sometimes happens,
even in the best of families,
that a baby is born.
This is not necessarily
cause for alarm.
The important thing
is to keep your wits
about you and
borrow some money.

—Elinor Goulding Smith
(1917–1978)
American writer and humorist

The hand that rocks the cradle is the hand that rules the world.

—William Ross Wallace
(1819–1881)
American poet

In the sheltered simplicity of the

first days after a baby is born,

one sees again the magical closed circle,

the miraculous sense of two people existing

only for each other, the tranquil sky

reflected on the face of the mother nursing the child.

—Anne Morrow Lindbergh

(1906–2001)

American writer and aviator

Biology is the least of what makes someone a mother.

—Oprah Winfrey

(b. 1954)

American TV host and actress

Childbirth is more

admirable than conquest,

more amazing than self-defense,

and as courageous as either one.

—Gloria Steinem

(b. 1934)

American writer and women's rights activist

Sweet dreams from a shade,

O'er my lovely infant's head.

Sweet dreams of pleasant streams,

By happy silent moony beams.

Sweet dreams with soft down,

Weave thy brows an infant crown.

Sweet sleep angel mild,

Hover o'er my happy child.

—from "A Cradle Song"

William Blake

(1757–1827)

British poet and artist

My only advice is to stay aware,

listen carefully and

yell for help if you need it.

—Judy Blume

(b. 1938)

American writer

Mothers are fonder than fathers of their children

because they are more certain they are their own.

—Aristotle

(384 B.C.–322 B.C.)

Greek philosopher

Making the decision to have
a child—it's momentous.
It is to decide forever to have
your heart go walking
around outside your body.

—Elizabeth Stone

(20th Century)

American journalist and author

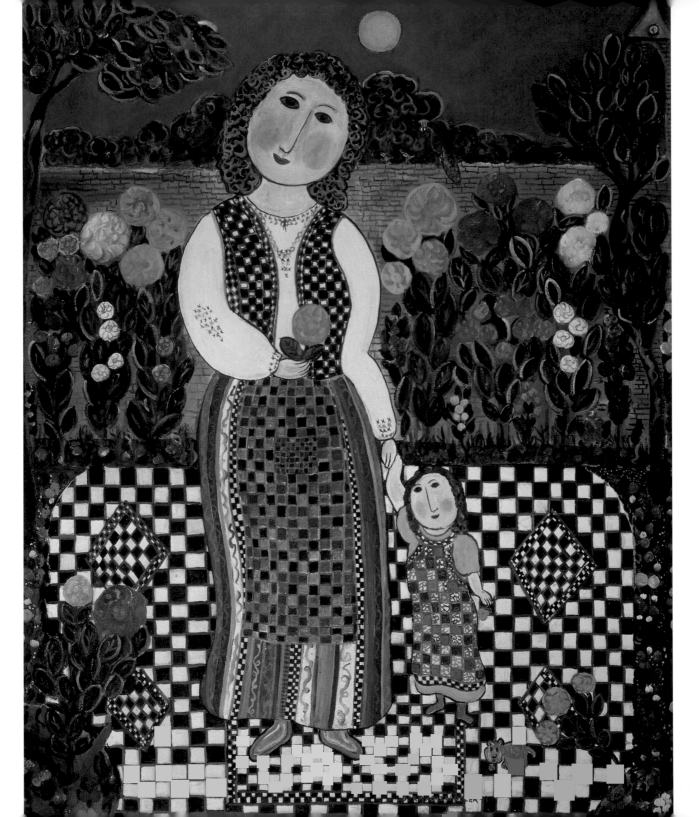

Let there be blue sunshine.
Let there be blue skies.
Let there be mama.
Let there be me.

—Russian folk song

Children

God could not be everywhere and therefore he made mothers.

—Jewish proverb

There is only one pretty child in the world, and every mother has it.

—Chinese proverb

More than any other human relationship, overwhelmingly more, motherhood means being instantly interruptible, responsive, responsible.

—Tillie Lerner Olsen

(b. 1913)

American writer

The mother's heart is the child's schoolroom.

—Henry Ward Beecher

(1813–1887)

American cleric

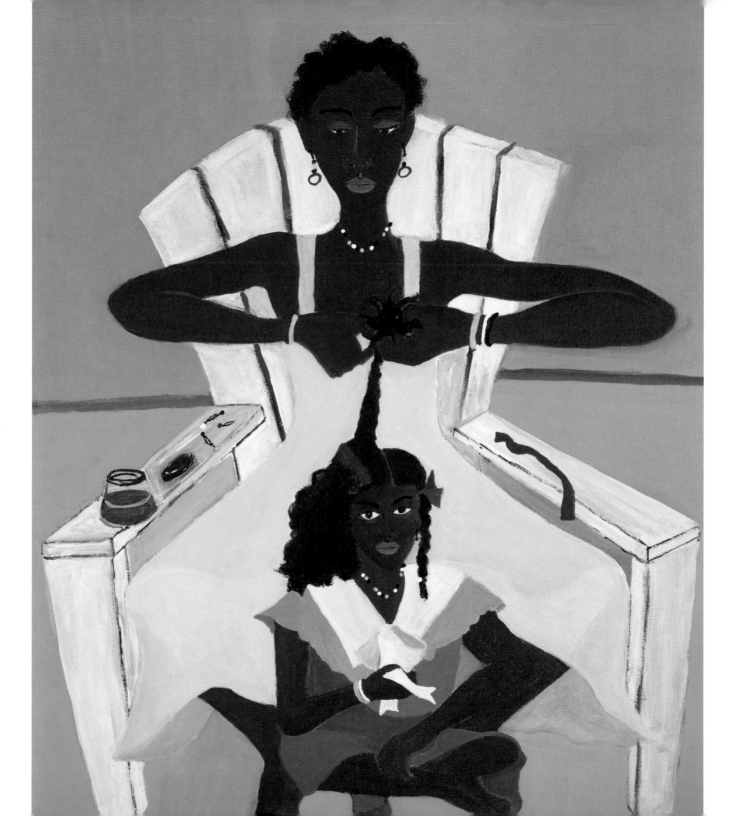

Motherhood—the second oldest profession and the biggest on-the-job training program.

—Erma Bombeck

(1927–1996)

American columnist and humorist

Before becoming a mother
I had a hundred theories
on how to bring up children.
Now I have seven children
and only one theory:
love them,
especially when they least deserve
to be loved.

—Kate Samperi

A woman who can cope with the terrible twos
can cope with anything.

—Unknown

Oh, what a power is motherhood, possessing
a potent spell
All women alike
fight fiercely for a child.

—from *Iphigenia at Aulis*

Euripides

(480?–406 B.C.)

Greek playwright

Bitter are the tears of a child: Sweeten them.

Deep are the thoughts of a child: Quiet them.

Sharp is the grief of a child: Take it from him.

Soft is the heart of a child: Do not harden it.

—Pamela Glenconner

(1871–1928)

British writer

By and large, mothers and housewives are the only workers who do not have regular time off. They are the great vacationless class.

—Anne Morrow Lindbergh

(1906–2001)

American writer and aviator

Everybody knows that a good mother gives her children a feeling of trust and stability. She is their earth. She is the one they can count on for the things that matter most of all. She is their food and their bed and the extra blanket when it grows cold in the night; she is their warmth and their health and their shelter; she is the one they want to be near when they cry. She is the only person in the whole world in a whole lifetime who can be these things to her children. There is no substitute for her. Somehow even her clothes feel different to her children's hands from anybody else's clothes. Only to touch her skirt or her sleeve makes a troubled child feel better.

—Katharine Butler Hathaway
(1890–1942)
American writer

One of the oldest human needs
is having someone to wonder when
you don't come home at night.

—Margaret Mead

(1901–1978)

American anthropologist

Women as the guardians of children possess a great power.

They are the moulders of their children's

personalities and the arbiters of their development.

—Ann Oakley

(b. 1944)

British sociologist and writer

The mother-child relationship is paradoxical and, in a sense, tragic. It requires the most intense love on the mother's side, yet this very love must help the child grow away from the mother, and to become fully independent.

—Erich Fromm

(1900–1980)

American psychoanalyst

Mother's love is peace.
It need not be acquired,
it need not be deserved.

—Erich Fromm

(1900–1980)

American psychoanalyst

God knows that **a mother needs** fortitude and courage and tolerance and flexibility and patience and firmness and nearly every other brave aspect of the human soul. But because I happen to be a parent of almost fiercely maternal nature, I praise casualness. It seems to me the rarest of virtues. It is useful enough when children are small. It is important to the point of necessity when they are adolescents.

—Phyllis McGinley
(1905–1978)
American poet
and essayist

Mama exhorted her children at every opportunity to "jump at de sun." We might not land on the sun, but at least we would get off the ground.

—Zora Neale Hurston

(1903–1960)

American writer and folklorist

The darn trouble with cleaning the house is
that it gets dirty the next day anyway,
so skip it a week if you have to.
The children are the most important thing.

—Barbara Bush

(b. 1925)

American first lady (1989–1993)

Her children arise up and call her blessed.

—Proverbs 31:28

The Bible

A **mother** is a person who seeing there are only four pieces of pie for five people, promptly announces she never did care for pie.

—Unknown

Sweater, n.: garment worn by child when its mother is feeling chilly.

—Ambrose Bierce

(1842–1914)

American journalist, satirist, and writer

Personal Reflection

Sometimes the strength of motherhood is greater than natural laws.

—Barbara Kingsolver

(b. 1955)

American writer

Mothers are the most instinctive philosophers.

—Harriet Beecher Stowe

(1811–1896)

American writer

We think back through our mothers if we are women.

—Virginia Woolf

(1882–1941)

British writer

No matter how old a mother is, she watches her middle-aged children for signs of improvement.

—Florida Scott-Maxwell

(1883–1979)

American writer and psychologist

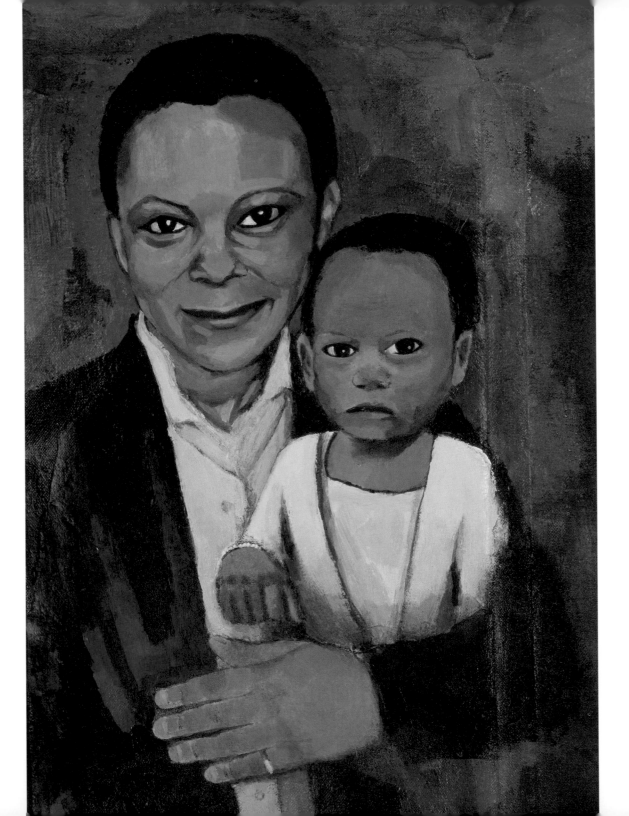

The mother is the most precious possessions of the nation, so precious that society advances its highest well-being when it protects the functions of the mother.

—Ellen Key

(1849–1926)

Swedish writer

Don't call me an icon.
I'm just a mother trying to help.

—Diana Spencer

(1961–1997)

Princess of Wales

Mothers have as powerful an influence over the welfare of future generations as all other earthly influences combined.

—John Stevens Cabot Abbott

(1805–1877)

American writer

Motherhood brings as much joy as ever, but it still brings boredom, exhaustion, and sorrow too. Nothing else ever will make you as happy or as sad, as proud or as tired, for nothing is quite as hard as helping a person develop his own individuality especially while you struggle to keep your own.

—Marguerite Kelly and Elia Parsons

(20th Century)

American writers

A mother is not a person to lean on, but a person to make leaning unnecessary.

—Dorothy Canfield Fisher

(1879–1958)

American writer

Mothers all want their sons to grow up to be President, but they don't want them to become politicians in the process.

—John F. Kennedy

(1917–1963)

35th president of the United States

Lord Illingworth: All women become like their mothers. That is their tragedy.

Mrs. Allonby: No man does. That is his.

—from *A Woman of No Importance*

Oscar Wilde

(1854–1900)

Irish wit, writer and playwright

The older I get
the more of my mother
I see in myself.

—Nancy Friday

(b. 1937)

American writer

Mother,

give

me

the sun.

— from *Ghosts*

Henrik Ibsen

(1828–1906)

Norwegian playwright

What do you do with all the antennae of motherhood when they become obsolete?

What do you do with the loose wires that dangle after eighteen

years of intimate connection to your own child?

What use is there for the expertise of motherhood that took so long to acquire?

—From "Caravan to College"

Ellen Goodman

(b. 1941)

American columnist

I would like them to be the happy end of my story.

—Margaret Atwood

(b. 1939)

Canadian writer

O.Bannion.

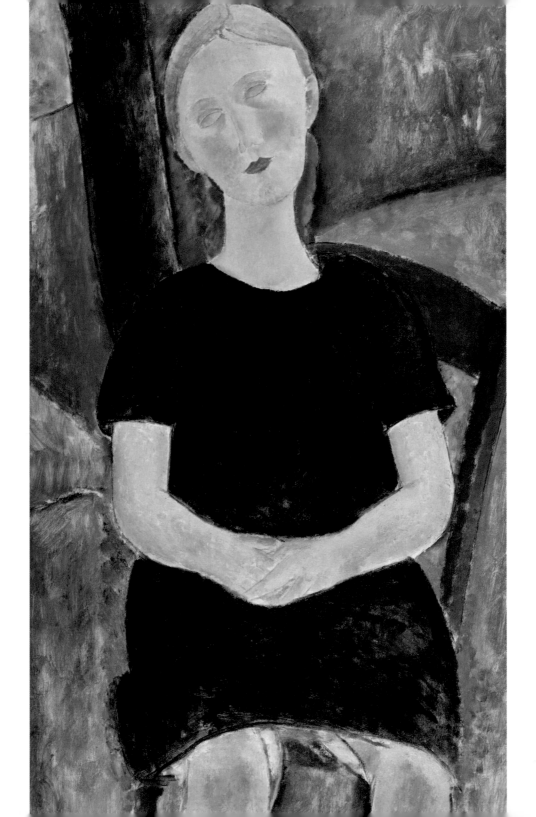

My mother always found me out.
Always. She's been dead for
thirty-five years, but I have this feeling
that even now she's watching.

—Natalie Babbitt

(b. 1932)

American writer

You have a wonderful child.

Then, when he's 13,

gremlins carry him away

and leave in his place

a stranger who gives you

not a moments peace.

—Jill Eikenberry

(b. 1947)

American actress

There never was a woman like her. She was gentle as a dove and brave as a lioness. . . .

The memory of my mother and her teachings were, after all,

the only capital I had to start life with, and on that capital I have made my way.

—Andrew Jackson

(1767–1845)

7th president of the United States

She is my first, great love.

She was a wonderful, rare woman—you do not know;

as strong, and steadfast, and generous as the sun.

She could be as swift as a white whiplash,

and as kind and gentle as warm rain,

and as steadfast as the irreducible earth beneath us.

—D.H. Lawrence

(1885–1930)

British writer

My mother was the making of me.

—Thomas Edison

(1847–1931)

American scientist

My mother was the most beautiful woman I ever saw. All I am I owe to my mother. I attribute all my success in life to the moral, intellectual and physical education I received from her.

—George Washington

(1732–1799)

1st president of the United States

The greatest lessons
I have ever learned were
at my mother's knees. . . .
All that I am, or hope to be,
I owe to my angel mother.

—Abraham Lincoln

(1809–1865)

16th president of the United States

I know how to do anything—I'm a mom.

—Roseanne Barr

(b. 1952)

American actress and comedian

Art Credits

Front cover: *Carefree* (ca. 1996), by Kelly Stribling Sutherland. Courtesy of the artist, www.uponepairofstairs.com.

Back cover: *She looks and looks, and still with new delight*, by James John Hill. Bonhams, London, UK/Bridgeman Art Library.

p. 9: *Waiting Woman* (1993), by Paul King. Courtesy of the artist.

p. 11: *Mother and Child, Sheep Meadow* (1990), by Bill Jacklin. Private collection/Bridgeman Art Library.

p. 12: *Watch the Stopper* (1991), by Jessie Coates. © Private collection/Jessie Coates/SuperStock.

p. 15: *Motherhood* (1952), by Leopold Presas. © Zurbaran Galeria, Buenos Aires/SuperStock.

p. 17: *Mother and Child* (1900), by Mary Stevenson Cassatt. © Brooklyn Museum of Art, New York, USA/ Bridgeman Art Library.

p. 18: *Le Berceau* or *The Cradle* (1872), by Berthe Morisot. The Art Archive/Musée D'Orsay, Paris/Dagli Orti.

p. 21: *Mother with Children* (20th century), by Ditz. Private collection/Bridgeman Art Library.

p. 22: *Mother and Child* (1903), by Paula Modersohn-Becker. Hamburg Kunsthalle, Hamburg, Germany/ Bridgeman Art Library.

p. 25: *Hepzibah's New Baby* (1985), by Dora Holzhandler. Private collection/Bridgeman Art Library.

p. 27: *The Three Ages of Woman*, detail (1905), by Gustav Klimt. © Gallery of Modern Art, Rome/The Art Archive, London/SuperStock.

p. 28: *Lord of the Manor* (1919), by Edmund Blair Leighton. © SuperStock.

p. 31: *Carefree* (ca. 1996), by Kelly Stribling Sutherland. Courtesy of the artist, www.uponepairofstairs.com.

p. 32: *Mother and Child in Autumn* (1998), by Dora Holzhandler. Private collection/Bridgeman Art Library.

p. 35: *Share the World* (1998), by Christian Pierre. © Christian Pierre/SuperStock.

p. 36: *Summer* (1999), by Zhang Shu Rong. © Super-Stock.

p. 39: *The Writing Lesson* (ca. 1905), by Pierre-Auguste Renoir. © Barnes Foundation, Merion, Pennsylvania/ SuperStock.

p. 40: *Braids* (1995), by Arnold Rice. © Private collection/Arnold Rice/SuperStock.

p. 43: *On the Dock* (1993), by Christian Pierre. © Christian Pierre/SuperStock.

p. 45: *Mother and Child* (1985), by Mahvash Mossaed. Courtesy of the artist, www.mahvashmossaed.com.

p. 47: *Can I Have the Bowl?* (1994), by Jessie Coates. © Private collection/Jessie Coates/SuperStock.

p. 48: *Mother and Child* (ca. 1904), by Paula Modersohn-Becker. Haags Gemeentemuseum, Netherlands/Bridgeman Art Library.

p. 51: *Brownstone Blues* (2000), by Francks Deceus. Private collection/Bridgeman Art Library.

p. 52: *The Stargazers* (1995), by Christian Pierre. © Private collection/Christian Pierre/SuperStock.

p. 55: *French Bouquet* (1891), by Paul Gauguin. © Pushkin Museum of Fine Arts, Moscow, Russian Federation/SuperStock.

p. 56: *The Flower* by Leslie Xuereb. © Leslie Xuereb/ SuperStock.

p. 59: *Communion Celebration* by Montas Antoine. © Private collection/Van Hoorick Fine Art/SuperStock.

p. 60: *Radmila and Claude Sutton* (1989), by Jacob Sutton. Private collection/Bridgeman Art Library.

p. 63: *Mother and Child* (20th century), by Ditz. Private collection/Bridgeman Art Library.

p. 64: *Earth Mother* (1882), by Edward Burne-Jones. © Bridgeman Art Library, London/SuperStock.

p. 67: *Picking Grapes* by Celeste Griswold. © Super-Stock.

p. 68: *Black Madonna X: Iris and Ephrem* (1999), by Elizabeth Barakah Hodges. © Elizabeth Barakah Hodges/SuperStock.

p. 71: *Dancing in the Rain* (1994), by Hui Shu Yi. © Red Lantern Folk Art/The Mukashi Collection/Super-Stock.

p. 72: *Like We Were Complete Strangers* (1994), by Mahvash Mossaed. Courtesy of the artist, www.mahvashmossaed.com.

p. 74: *Woman with Little Boy Reaching for a Persimmon* (1906), by Houn. © Culver Pictures Inc./SuperStock.

p. 77: *Mother and Child in the Park* by Auguste Macke. © SuperStock.

p. 78: *Afternoon of the Children at Wargemont* (1884), by Pierre-August Rodin. © National Gallery, Berlin/Super-Stock.

p. 81: *She looks and looks, and still with new delight*, by James John Hill. Bonhams, London, UK/Bridgeman Art Library.

p. 82: *Retablo Para Mi Hermana Rosario Sánchez Cardenas* (1994), by Marta Sánchez. Courtesy of Bill and Kathy Kulik.

p. 85: *Dance Around the Tree* by B.O. Bannion. © Super-Stock.

p. 86: Untitled (portrait of a woman), by Amedeo Modigliani. © Solomon R. Guggenheim Museum, New York/SuperStock.

p. 89: *Daughter of the Rainbow* (1996), by Daniel Nevins. © Daniel Nevins/SuperStock.

p. 90: *Mother and Child* by Diana Ong. © Diana Ong/ SuperStock.

p. 93: *Woman and Child* (ca. 1810), by Follower of Sir Thomas Lawrence. © The Huntington Library, Art Collections, and Botanical Gardens, San Marino, California/SuperStock.

p. 94: *Mama's Helper* (1998), by Kelly Stribling Sutherland. Courtesy of the artist, www.uponepairofstairs.